Help with Homework

Science

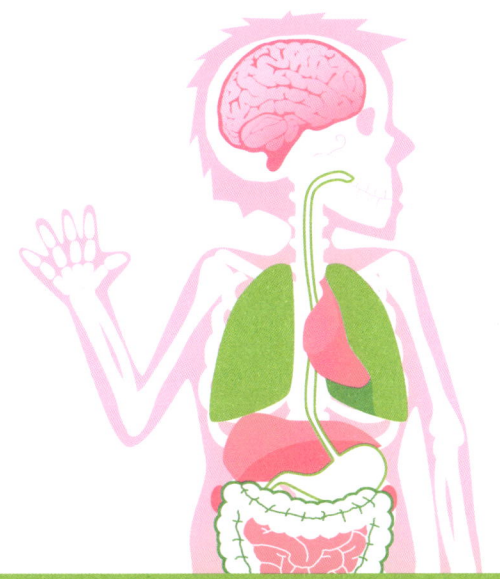

Here's a short note to parents:
These fun activities are designed to supplement the science teaching taught in primary school, to introduce first concepts and build up your child's knowledge of science. It is recommended that you spend time with your child while doing any kind of school practice, to offer encouragement and guidance. Most of all, we hope you enjoy sharing this book together!

Written by Nina Filipek
Designed and illustrated by Jeannette O'Toole
Cover design by Dan Green

Autumn Publishing

www.autumnchildrensbooks.co.uk

Is it a living thing?

A doll and a child are very different –
the child is a living thing but the doll is not.
Draw lines from these descriptions to the pictures.
You can draw more than one line to some things.

can move by itself

can grow

can use its senses

can breathe
or respire

can eat food

child

toy car

plant

doll

dog

bird

Place your
star sticker
here

Which of these are living things?
Which of these are not living things?
Colour the living things.

Green fingers!

All living plants need some basic things in order to grow.
Colour in the things that living plants need.

water

sunlight

electricity

warmth

clothes

food

Which things do they not need? Cross them out.

Staying alive

Find the stickers and put them in place. Tick **A** or **B** each time.

1. Which seeds will germinate?

 seeds **A**

in the refrigerator

 seeds **B**

in a warm place

2. Which seedling will grow fastest?

 seedling **A**

on a sunny windowsill

 seedling **B**

in a dark cupboard

3. Which plant will continue to grow?

 plant **A**

given no water

 plant **B**

given a little water every day

4. Which plant will reproduce and make new plants?

 plant **A**

it has flowers and seeds

 plant **B**

it has no flowers or seeds

Science dictionary
Germinate – when a seed starts to grow.

Place your star sticker here

Plant parts

Label the different parts of this plant. Choose from the following words:

leaves   stem   roots   flowers   seeds   pollen   plants

Choose from the same words to complete the sentences.

1. The _____ hold the plant firmly in the ground.

2. Nutrients from the soil travel through the roots, up the _____ and to the leaves.

3. The _____ soak up sunlight and convert it into energy and food for the plant.

4. The _____ attract insects that feed on the pollen.

5. The _____ sticks to the insects and is spread to other plants.

6. The flowers die and _____ are formed.

7. The seeds are scattered and grow to make new _____.

Science dictionary

Photosynthesis – the process of the leaves soaking up sunlight and converting it into energy and food.

Pollinator – an animal or an insect that spreads pollen from one plant to another.

Place your star sticker here

What's for dinner?

All living things are part of what is called a 'food chain'.
Plants are at the beginning of every food chain.
Follow the arrows in this food chain to see who eats what.

plants → fish → heron

➡ means 'eaten by'

Draw a food chain for each group of living things below.
Put the living things in order of who eats what.

1. **mouse   owl   plants**

   ☐ ➡ ☐ ➡ ☐

2. **lion   plants   zebra**

   ☐ ➡ ☐ ➡ ☐

3. **insects   snake   frog   plants**

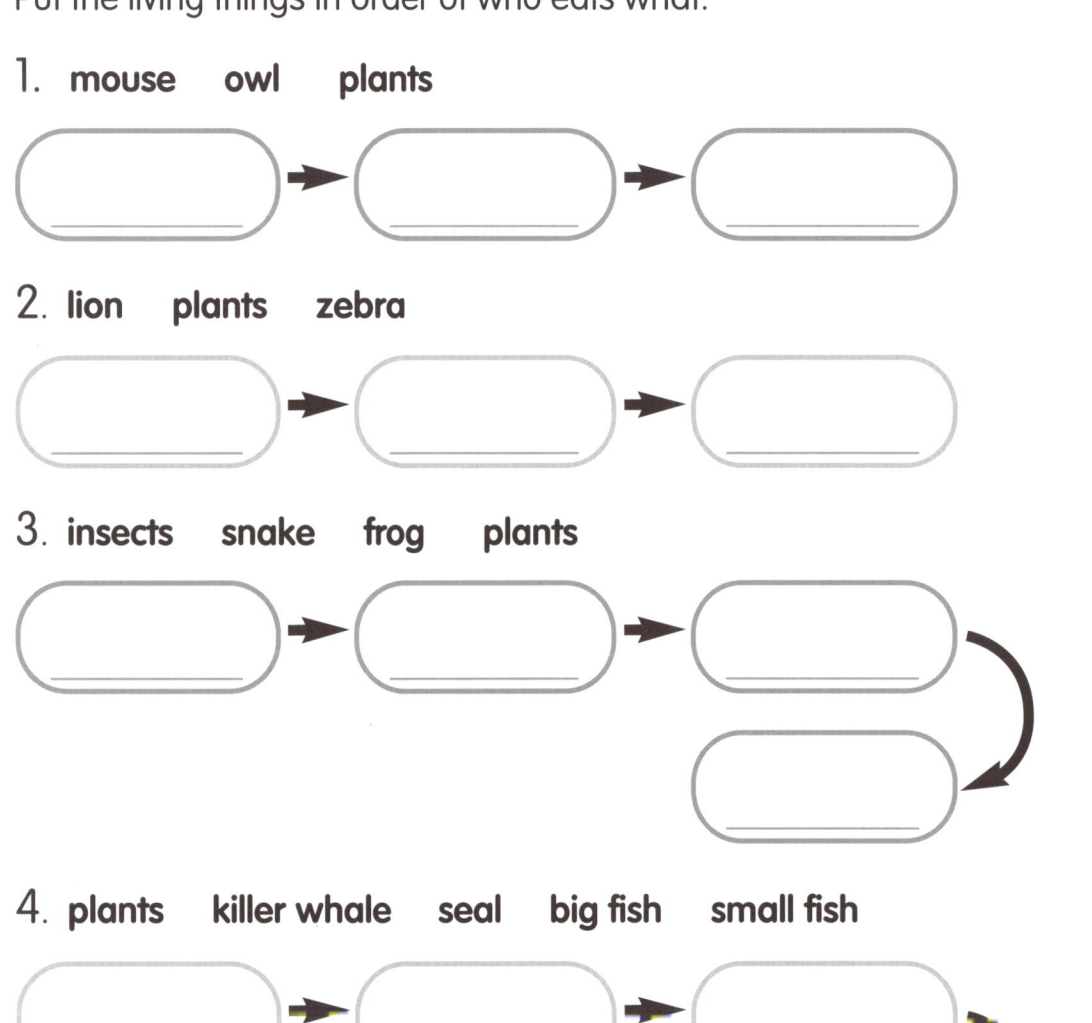

4. **plants   killer whale   seal   big fish   small fish**

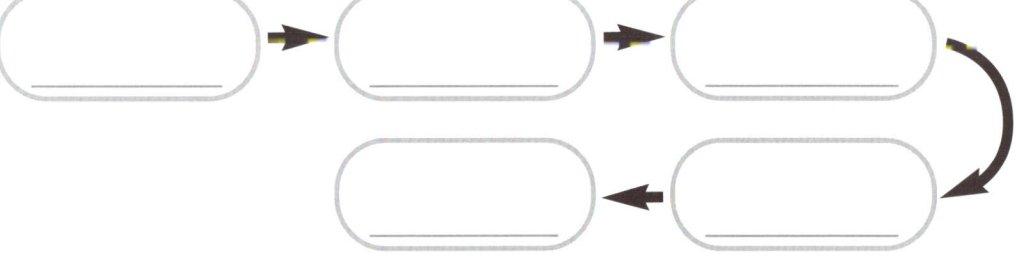

Place your
star sticker
here

Predator or prey?

'Predators' are animals that eat other animals.
'Prey' are the animals they eat.

Find the stickers and put them in place.
Circle the predator in each pair of animal words.

wolf   –   bison

Place your
sticker here

shark   –   sea turtle

slug   –   hedgehog

blackbird   –   earthworm

vole   –   owl

seal   –   polar bear

Place your
sticker here

tiger   –   deer

small snake   –   eagle

Place your
star sticker
here

Adapting

All plants and animals are adapted to where they live.
Find the stickers and put them in place. Draw a line to join each animal or plant to its special features or adaptations.

shark

thick stem and leaves to store water

Place your sticker here
tree frog

brightly coloured to scare predators

horns to defend itself from predators

cactus

webbed feet, streamlined body for swimming

rows of razor-sharp teeth to catch prey

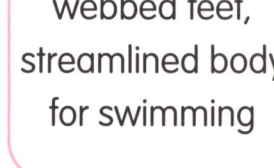
tiger

seal

long sticky tongue to catch insects

stripes provide camouflage in the long grass

rhinoceros

Place your sticker here
chameleon

Place your star sticker here

Classifying

Write the names of these animals in the correct groups below.

**frog   lizard   toad   tortoise   crocodile   snake
human   whale   raven   rabbit   beetle   trout
pike   shark   owl   swan   penguin   housefly   dog**

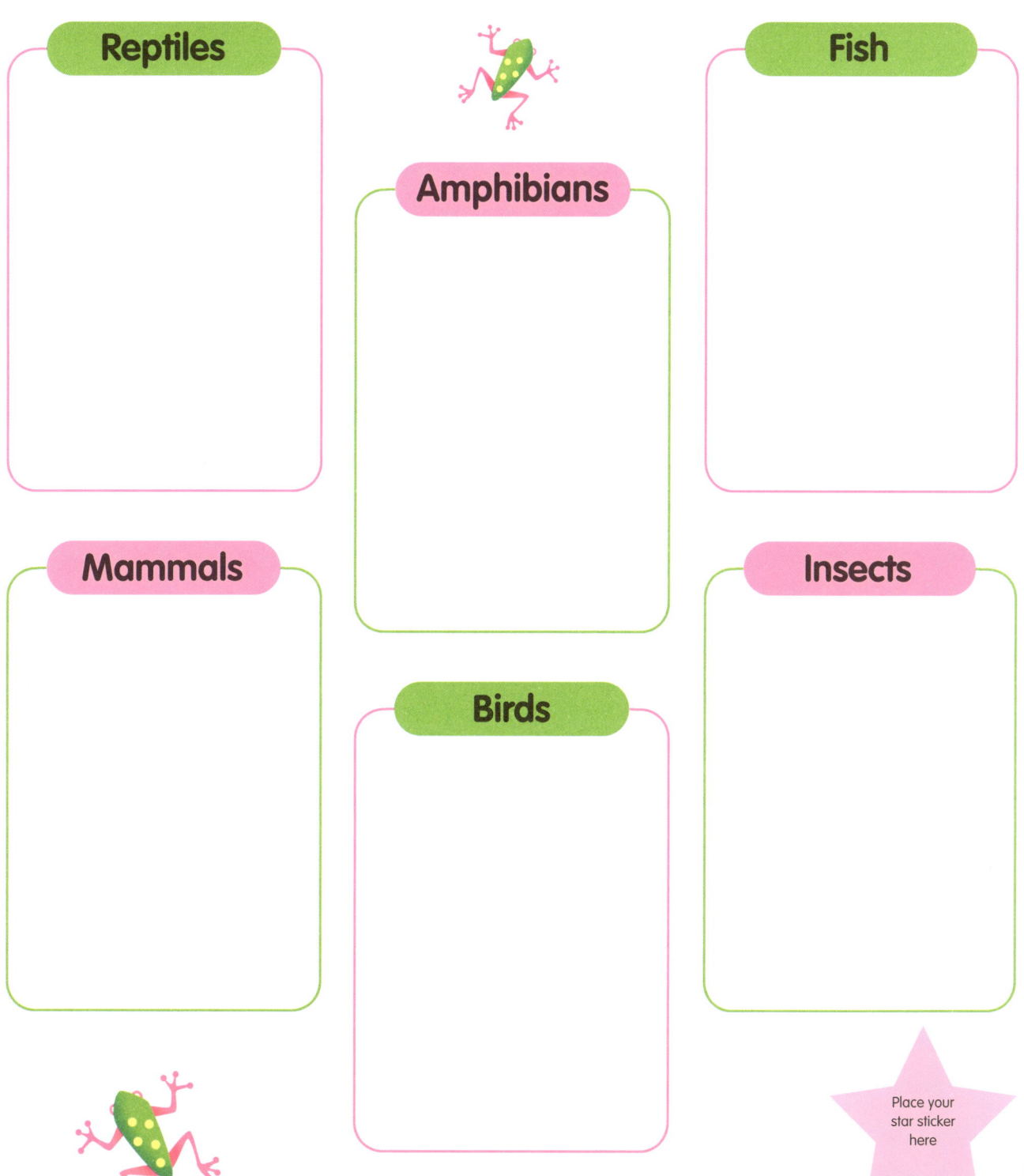

Reptiles

Fish

Amphibians

Mammals

Insects

Birds

Place your
star sticker
here

Human body

Your body is working the whole time – even when you are sleeping. Learn the names of these important parts of your body and read about what they do.

Find the sticker and put it in place. Label the different parts of the body.
Write on the lines, choosing from the words below.

heart lungs brain stomach bladder kidneys intestines liver

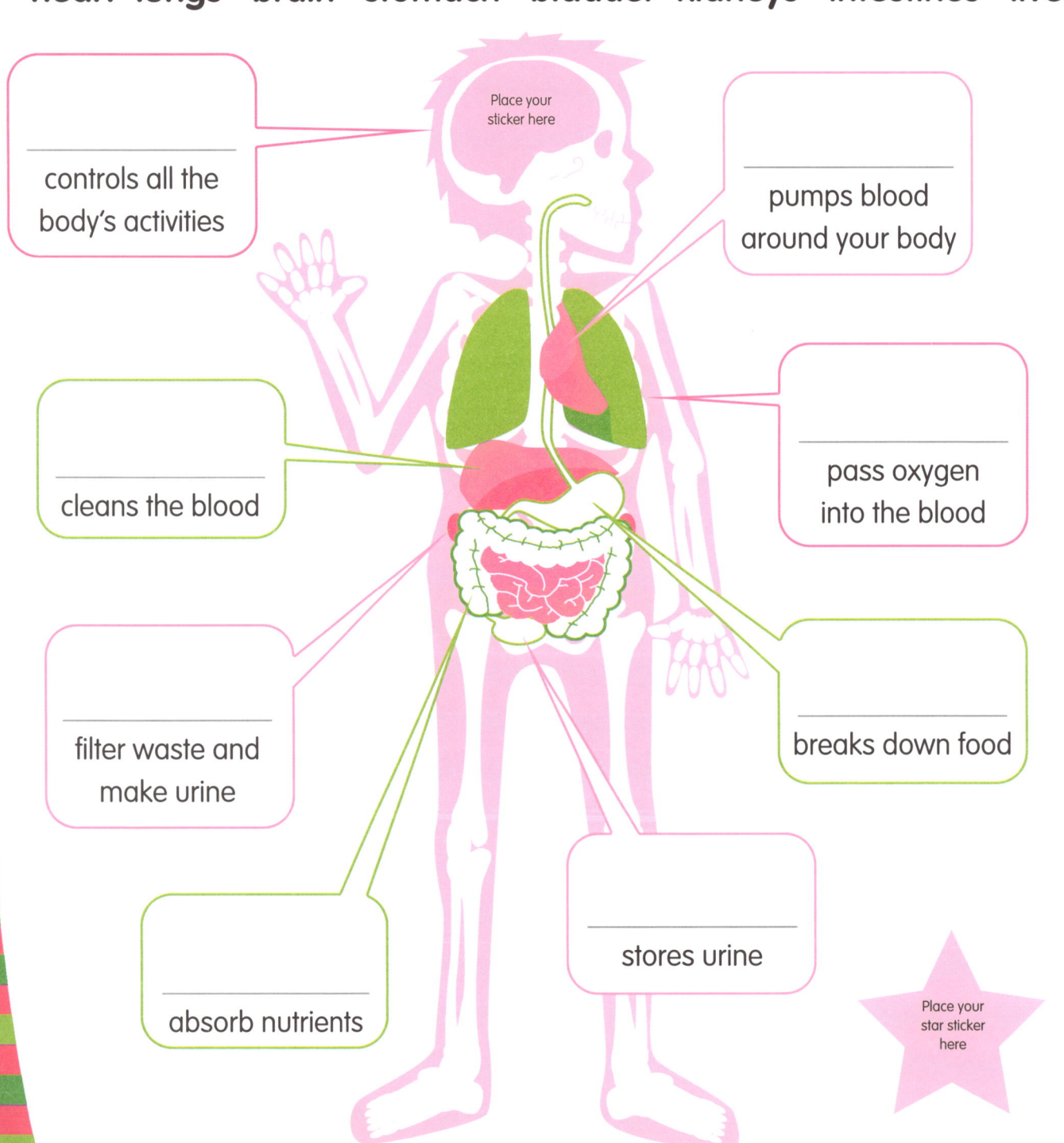

controls all the body's activities

Place your sticker here

pumps blood around your body

cleans the blood

pass oxygen into the blood

filter waste and make urine

breaks down food

absorb nutrients

stores urine

Place your star sticker here

Skin and bones

Your skin has many different jobs.

Circle the things your skin does for you. Cross out the things it does not do.

It keeps germs out.

It regulates my body temperature.

It pumps blood.

It produces vitamin D.

It protects what's inside my body.

It helps me breathe.

It senses pain, touch, temperature.

It digests food.

Fill in the missing words to complete these facts about your skeleton.

skull   skeleton   spine   femur   feet   ribs

1. There are 206 bones in the human _____.

2. The bone that protects your brain is called your _____.

3. The bones in your back are called your _____.

4. The bones in your chest are called your _____.

5. The longest bone in your body is your _____.

6. Most of your bones are in your _____.

Place your star sticker here

Eat well

Having a healthy diet means eating a variety of foods from each food group every day.

Write these foods in the correct food groups below:

**butter   fish   oranges   rice   broccoli   peas
yoghurt   pasta   tomatoes   cream**

Carbohydrates

potatoes   cereals
noodles   bread

Fruit and vegetables

apples   bananas
carrots   green beans

Proteins

meat   beans   milk
cheese   eggs

Dairy products

milk   cheese

Draw a healthy plate of food, including foods from each food group.

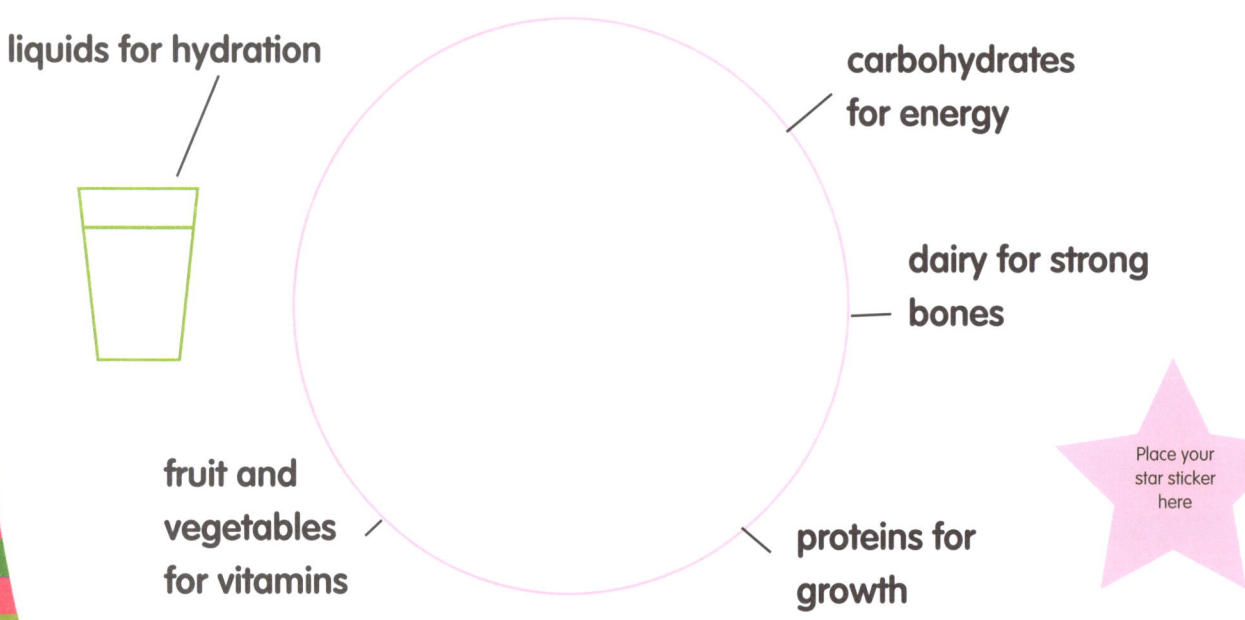

liquids for hydration

carbohydrates
for energy

dairy for strong
bones

fruit and
vegetables
for vitamins

proteins for
growth

Teeth

We have 26 baby teeth (or first teeth). We lose these from the age of about five years to make way for our 32 permanent (or second) teeth.

Draw each of your teeth in the correct place on the upper and lower jaw below. Use a hand mirror (or photograph) to help you do this.

We need to look after our teeth in order to stay healthy. Write some rules for caring for your teeth. Try to use these words:

twice a day, toothbrush, toothpaste, floss, plaque, sugary snacks, fizzy drinks, dentist, check-ups

1._____

_____

2._____

_____

3._____

_____

4._____

_____

Count and then complete the following:

I have _____ baby teeth.

I have _____ permanent teeth.

I have _____ gaps.

Your back teeth are called **molars**, your pointy teeth are **canines** and your front teeth are **incisors**. Label these on your drawing above.

Place your star sticker here

Material world

A material is what something is made of. Materials have features (called 'properties') that make them useful for particular products.

Complete the table below. Think about how the following materials are used. Look around your home for examples.

Material	Properties	Used for:
wool	warm, soft, can be knitted and woven	clothes
steel	strong, hard	
rubber	flexible, can be moulded	
glass	transparent	
plastic	flexible, can be moulded	
paper	flexible, lightweight	
stone	strong, hard	

What's it made of?

Find the stickers and put them in place. Then write on the lines why each material is suitable for making each product.

pottery _____

fabric _____

Place your sticker here

leather _____

glass _____

wood _____

Place your sticker here

aluminium _____

rubber _____

Place your star sticker here

Be a scientist!

Scientists are people who ask questions about the world around them. They think about what will happen in certain situations and make predictions. Then they test their ideas to see if they were right. You can be a scientist, too, by investigating the following question:

Which materials will float?

What you need:

bucket of water

small objects made of the following materials –
wood (small stick)
rubber (eraser)
modelling clay
steel (cutlery)
pottery (plate)
polystyrene (packaging)

What you do:

1. Predict whether you think each object will float or sink. Complete the table below.

2. Find out if you were right by putting the objects in a sink or bucket filled with water.

3. Record your results in the table below.

4. Explain what happened and why you think this happened.

5. Test two more items of your own choice and complete the table with your findings.

Material	I predict it will... (float / sink)	Floats	Sinks	Explain why
wood				
rubber				
modelling clay				
steel				
pottery				
polystyrene				

Try this…

Shape the modelling clay so that it will float on water. Try a boat shape with sides to stop the water flooding in!

Place your sticker here

Place your star sticker here

Answer the following question by setting up your own science investigation:

Which materials are magnetic?

What you need:

magnet

objects made of different materials, for example –

copper coin
wooden spoon
steel paper clip
elastic band
paper

metal key
aluminium foil
iron nail
fabric toy

What you do:

1. Predict whether you think each object will be attracted to the magnet. Complete the table below.

2. Find out if you were right by testing each of the objects in turn. If the object sticks to the magnet then it is 'magnetic'.

3. Record your results in the table below.

4. Explain what happened and why you think this happened.

5. Test two more items of your own choice and complete the table with your findings.

Material	I predict it will (stick / not stick) to the magnet	Magnetic	Non-magnetic	Explain why
fabric				
wood				
paper				
plastic				
iron				
steel				

Try this…

You will need two bar magnets. Test them as below.

A | N | S | | S | N | ☐

B | N | S | | N | S | ☐

Which of these bar magnets will attract each other?
Tick A or B.

Solid or liquid?

Materials can be either a solid, or a liquid, or a gas.

For example:

Ice is a solid.   Water is a liquid.   Steam is a gas.

Find the stickers and put them in place. Draw lines to label the following items. Decide whether they are a solid, liquid or gas.

Place your sticker here

ice lolly

orange drink

banana

salt

solid

liquid

gas

Place your sticker here

chocolate bar

oxygen

clouds

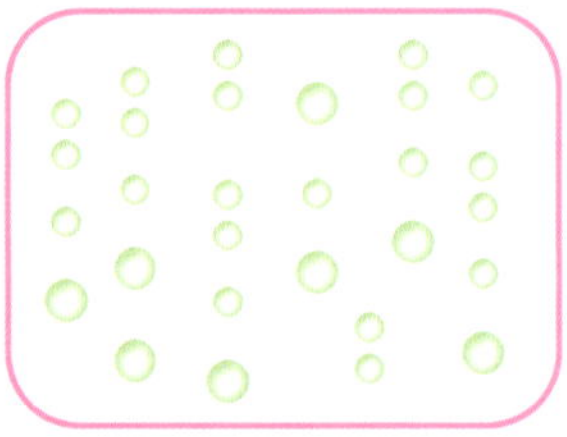

bubbles in
a fizzy drink

rainwater

We can turn some solids into liquids by heating them.

For example:

If we melt a chocolate bar it turns into a liquid.

If we cool it down again, it turns back into a solid!

Place your
star sticker
here

Water cycle

The water on our planet has been recycled over and over again throughout time. The water in your tap could be the same water that the dinosaurs drank from lakes millions of years ago!

Water is recycled through the 'water cycle'. Choose from the following words to complete this description of the water cycle.

rivers water clouds snow Sun evaporates wind rain

The _____ heats up the water in the oceans, lakes, _____ and streams and it evaporates. As it _____, it rises and then cools to form _____. The clouds are blown by the _____ over higher ground and are cooled even more. The droplets of _____ in the clouds get bigger and fall as _____ . If the air temperature is very cold, rain turns to _____ and ice.

Science dictionary
Evaporation – when a liquid turns into a gas
(e.g. water becomes water vapour)
Condensation – when a gas turns into a liquid
(e.g. water vapour becomes clouds)
Freezing – when a liquid turns into a solid
(e.g. water becomes ice)

Place your star sticker here

Be a scientist!

Investigate the following question using your science skills.

Which solids will dissolve in water?

What you need:

solids to test –
sugar, salt, flour, instant coffee, sand

teaspoon

beaker of water

beaker of warm water

What you do:

1. Put a teaspoon of the first solid you are going to test into the beaker of water.

2. Stir many times. Count and note the number of stirs in the table below.

3. Has the solid dissolved (broken up) in the water?

4. Record your results in the table.

5. Repeat the experiment but this time use warmer water. Does this make a difference?

6. Test the other solids from the list. Compare your findings.

Solid type	Number of stirs	Dissolves	Does not dissolve
sugar			
salt			
flour			
instant coffee			
sand			

Science dictionary

Solution – when a solid dissolves in water it makes a 'solution'.

Soluble – solids that dissolve in water.

Insoluble – solids that do not dissolve in water.

Place your star sticker here

Hear that?

Sounds are made when objects vibrate.
When you bang on a drum, the drum skin vibrates and sound waves travel through the air to reach your ears.

Make a list of sounds you can hear in your home and sounds you can hear outside. What made these sounds?

Sounds heard inside the house:	Sounds heard outside the house:

Sounds can travel through solids such as bricks, wood and glass. That's why we can hear sounds coming from outside the house.

Try this...

1. Rest the side of your head on top of a table so that your ear is resting against the surface.

2. Knock on top of the table.

3. Now lift up your head and knock on the table again.

Was the sound louder when you had your ear against the table? Why? The sound vibrations travelled more easily through the table than through the air – that's why the sound was louder.

Place your star sticker here

Light

Light comes from many sources.
Find the stickers and put them in place.
Circle the things that give us light.

Finish the sentences below by filling in the missing words.
Choose from the list.

electric   Sun   light   night-time   dark   Earth

1. The _____ gives us _____ throughout the day.

2. When the _____ turns away from the Sun we get

_____.

3. We switch on _____ lights in our homes

when it goes _____.

Place your
star sticker
here

Shade

Shadows are made when an object blocks out the light.

For example, the mug casts a shadow on the table because it blocks out the light from the lamp.

The shadows are missing from the pictures below! Where should the shadows be? You can draw them in. Look at the position of the Sun each time. The first one has been done for you.

Place your sticker here

Now you can colour in the pictures!

Have you noticed…?
Shadows are longest earlier in the morning and later in the day when the Sun appears lower in the sky. Shadows are shortest at midday.

Place your star sticker here

Push and pull

All movement is either a push or a pull force.

Find the stickers and put them in place. Label the following pictures.

Write push or pull under each one.

Place your sticker here

_____   _____   _____

Place your sticker here

_____

Now draw an arrow to show the direction of the force (or movement) in each picture.

Think of some more examples of pushes and pulls. Draw pictures of pushes and pulls in the space below. Then draw arrows to show the direction of the force in each example.

Place your star sticker here

Gravity pulls

A force called 'gravity' pulls all objects down to the Earth. The amount it pulls down is measured by the weight of the object.

Scientists measure weight in Newtons – named after Sir Isaac Newton the scientist who discovered how gravity works.

How much do you weigh in grams?
Write it here _____

100 grams equals 1 Newton.

Divide your weight in grams by 100 to calculate your weight in Newtons.

How much do you weigh in Newtons?
Write it here _____

Find out…
What would you weigh on the Moon? The pull of gravity on the Moon is six times less than on Earth. Divide your weight by six to find out what you would weigh on the Moon.

On the Moon I would weigh _____ grams.

Science dictionary
Weightlessness – astronauts experience 'weightlessness' in atmospheres that have no gravity.

Place your star sticker here

Air pushes

Air pushes up against falling objects to slow them down – this is called 'air resistance'.

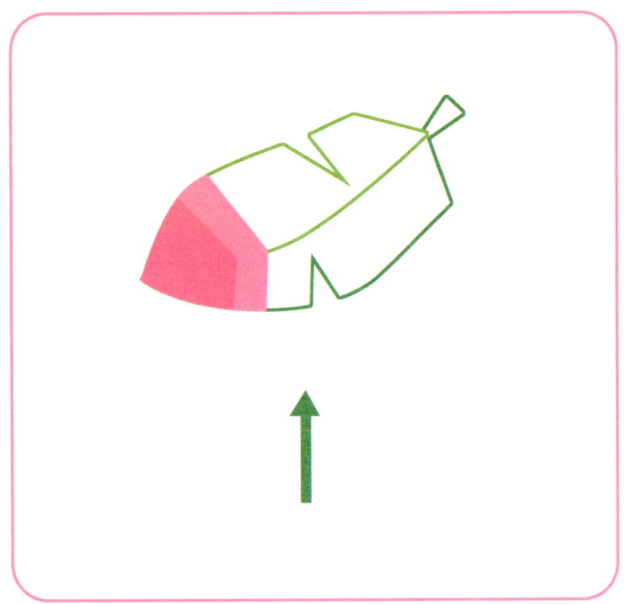

Place your sticker here

Find the sticker and put it in place. Draw an arrow to show the direction of the air resistance that slows down the parachute.

Some objects have a smooth streamlined shape to reduce air resistance. They often have a pointy shape at the front to cut through the air more easily.

Colour in the objects that have a streamlined shape.

Place your star sticker here

Friction

Another force called 'friction' tries to stop objects from moving over each other.

The man tries to push the heavy wardrobe across the floor but friction from the floor's surface stops the wardrobe from moving.

Draw an arrow to show the direction of the friction force that tries to stop this box from moving.

Some surfaces have high friction – they are bumpy and rough, while other surfaces have low friction – they are slippery and smooth.

Draw a line to label each surface as either 'high friction' or 'low friction':

sandy beach

high friction

ice-skating rink

ski slope

low friction

muddy field

Place your star sticker here

Be a scientist!

Use your science skills to find out how water pushes up against floating objects. This is called 'upthrust'.

Can you sink a plastic bottle?

What you need:

an empty plastic bottle (with top)

a bucket or sink of water

What you do:

1. Put the top on the bottle. Place it in the bucket or the sink and try to 'sink' it. What happens and why?

2. Half-fill the bottle with water. Try again. What happens now?

3. How full does the bottle need to be before it will sink? Why?

Find out…
How a submarine is able to sink to the bottom of the ocean and then rise to the surface again.

Place your star sticker here

Ship shape

Many sea creatures have a streamlined shape to help them move more easily through the water.

Find the sticker and put it in place. Colour and identify these streamlined sea creatures.

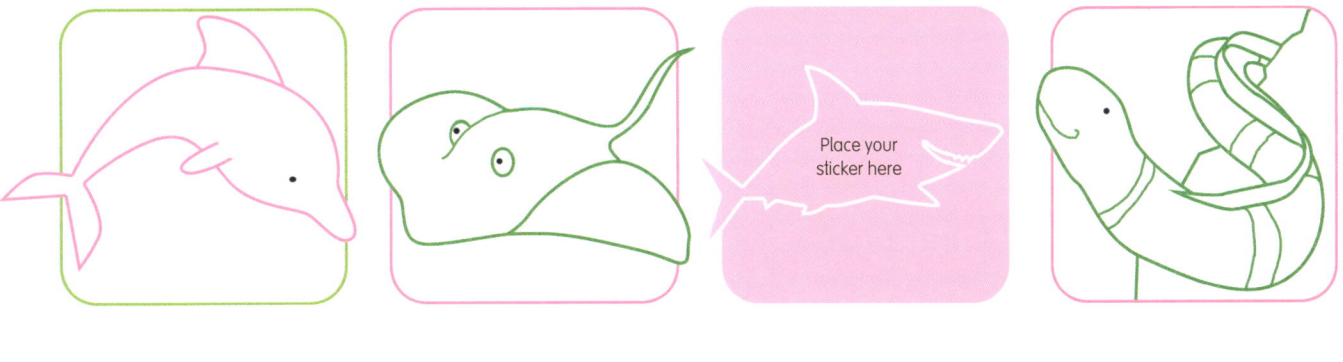

Place your sticker here

_____   _____   _____   _____

Which of these shapes is the best shape for a boat? Colour it in and add a sail.

A

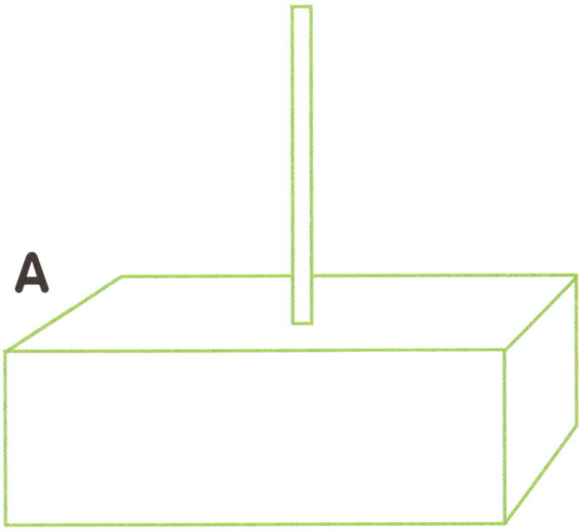

B

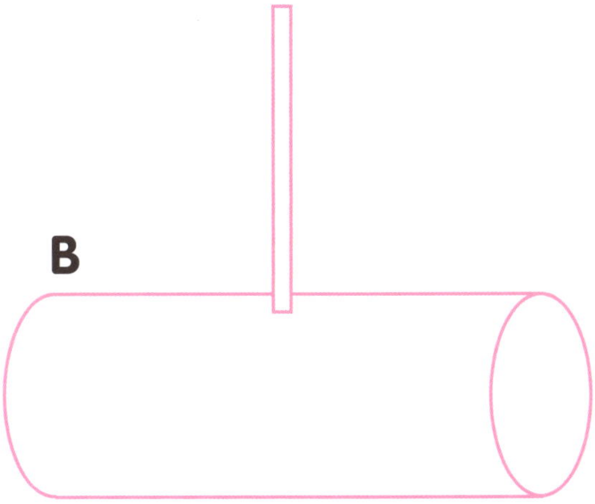

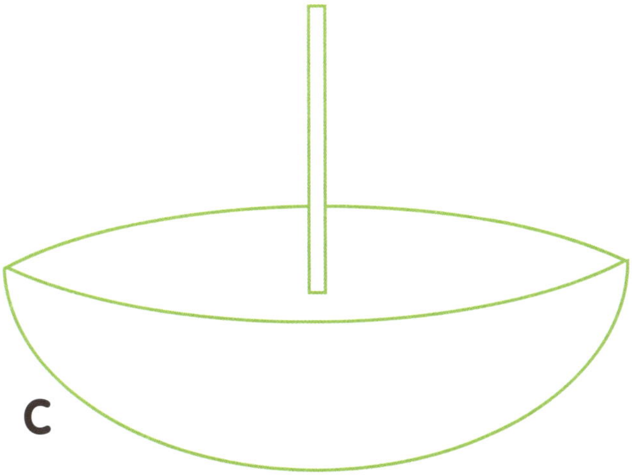

C

Place your star sticker here

In orbit

It takes the Earth one year to orbit (move around) the Sun. It takes the Moon one month to orbit the Earth. The Earth and the Moon both move in an anti-clockwise direction.

Label the Sun, the Moon and the Earth in the diagram below. Draw arrows to show the direction in which they move (anti-clockwise).

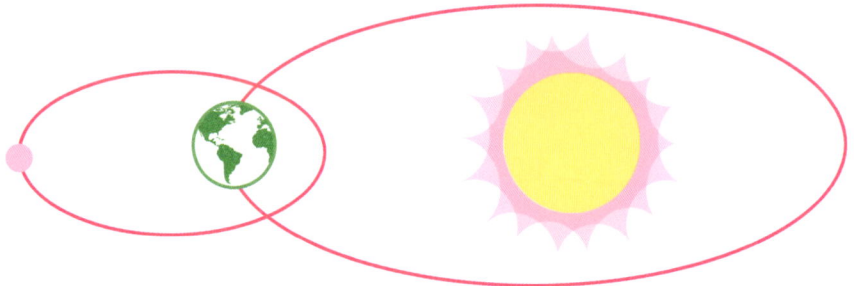

Fill in the missing words to complete the facts below.
Choose from the following words:

hours   day   night   spins   Earth

The Earth _____ at an angle on an invisible axis. It takes the Earth 24 _____ to turn once on its axis. This gives us _____ and night. The part of the _____ that turns towards the Sun has daytime. The part of the Earth that turns away from the Sun has _____ -time.

Shade the part of the Earth that is in darkness (night-time).

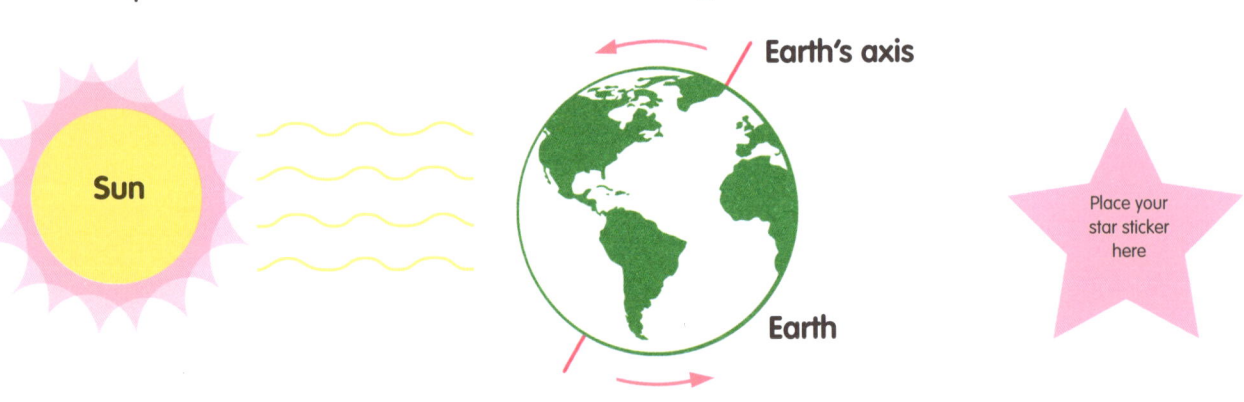

Sun

Earth's axis

Earth

Place your star sticker here

Answers

Is it a living thing?

can move by itself – child, plant (can turn to face the Sun), dog, bird
can grow – child, plant, dog, bird
can eat food – child, plant (leaves and roots take in food), dog, bird
can use its senses – child, plant (senses light), dog, bird
can breathe or respire – child, plant, dog, bird
The child, plant, dog and bird are living things.

Green fingers!

Living plants need these basic things in order to grow: **sunlight, warmth, water** and **food**. They do not need clothes and electricity.

Staying alive

1. **B**, 2. **A**, 3. **B**, 4. **A**

Plant parts

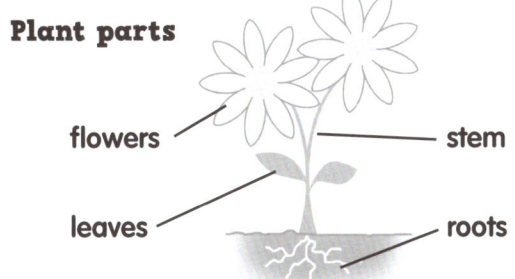

flowers
stem
leaves
roots

1. The **roots** hold the plant firmly in the ground.
2. Nutrients from the soil travel through the roots, up the **stem** and to the **leaves**.
3. The **leaves** soak up sunlight and convert it into energy and food for the plant.
4. The **flowers** attract insects that feed on the pollen.
5. The **pollen** sticks to the insects and is spread to other plants.
6. The flowers die and **seeds** are formed.
7. The seeds are scattered and grow to make new **plants**.

What's for dinner?

1. plants ➔ mouse ➔ owl
2. plants ➔ zebra ➔ lion
3. plants ➔ insects ➔ frog ➔ snake
4. plants ➔ small fish ➔ big fish ➔ seal ➔ killer whale

Predator or prey?

The predators are: wolf, shark, hedgehog, blackbird, owl, polar bear, tiger, eagle.

Adapting

shark – rows of razor-sharp teeth to catch prey
tree frog – brightly coloured to scare predators
cactus – thick stem and leaves to store water
tiger – stripes provide camouflage in the long grass
seal – webbed feet, streamlined body for swimming
rhinoceros – horns to defend itself from predators
chameleon – long sticky tongue to catch insects

Classifying

Reptiles – lizard, tortoise, crocodile, snake
Amphibians – frog, toad
Fish – trout, pike, shark
Mammals – human, whale, rabbit, dog
Birds – penguin, swan, raven, owl
Insects – beetle, housefly

Human body

brain – controls all the body's activities
heart – pumps blood around your body
lungs – pass oxygen into the blood
liver – cleans the blood
stomach – breaks down food
intestines – absorb nutrients
kidneys – filter waste and make urine
bladder – stores urine

Skin and bones

Your skin – keeps germs out, regulates your body temperature, protects what's inside your body, produces vitamin D, and senses pain, touch and temperature. It does not help you to breathe, pump blood or digest food.

1. There are 206 bones in the human **skeleton**.
2. The bone that protects your brain is called your **skull**.
3. The bones in your back are called your **spine**.
4. The bones in your chest are called your **ribs**.
5. The longest bone in your body is your **femur**.
6. Most of your bones are in your **feet**.

Eat well

Carbohydrates –
potatoes, cereals, noodles, bread, pasta, rice
Fruit and vegetables –
apples, bananas, carrots, green beans, oranges, broccoli, peas, tomatoes
Proteins – meat, beans, milk, cheese, fish, eggs
Dairy products – milk, cheese, butter, yoghurt, cream

Teeth Possible answers:
1. Brush twice a day using a clean toothbrush and toothpaste.
2. Use floss to remove food and plaque between your teeth.
3. Avoid too many sugary snacks and fizzy drinks.
4. Visit the dentist for regular check-ups.

Answers (contd)

Material world Possible answers:
wool is used for clothes, blankets
steel is used for cutlery, building and construction
rubber is used for tyres, balloons, elastic, wetsuits
glass is used for windows, ornaments
plastic is used for household items
paper is used for books, newspapers, greetings cards
stone is used for paving, buildings, statues

What's it made of? Possible answers:
pottery – waterproof, lightweight, can be moulded
fabric – soft, warm, flexible
leather – fairly waterproof, soft, warm, flexible
glass – transparent, smooth, can be moulded
wood – strong, lightweight
aluminium – lightweight, does not rust
rubber – elastic, can be moulded, hard-wearing

Which materials will float?
You should find that wood and polystyrene will float in water because they are lighter than the surrounding water. Rubber, clay, steel and pottery will sink because they are heavier than water. However, modelling clay will float if shaped into a 'boat'. (Heavy iron ships float because the weight of the water they displace is equal to their weight.)

Which materials are magnetic?
Objects made of iron and steel are magnetic. Wood, plastic, rubber, paper, and metals such as aluminium, silver, gold and copper are non-magnetic.
Magnet pair **B** will attract each other.
Like (same) poles repel.
Unlike (opposite) poles attract.

Solid or liquid?
Solid – ice lolly, banana, salt, chocolate bar
Liquid – orange drink, rainwater, clouds
Gas – oxygen, bubbles in a fizzy drink

Water cycle
The **Sun** heats up the water in the oceans, lakes, **rivers** and streams and it evaporates. As it **evaporates,** it rises and then cools to form **clouds**. The clouds are blown by the **wind** over higher ground and are cooled even more. The droplets of **water** in the clouds get bigger and fall as **rain**. If the air temperature is very cold, rain turns to **snow** and ice.

Which solids will dissolve in water?
Sugar, salt and instant coffee will dissolve in water. Flour will partially dissolve. Most solids dissolve faster in warmer water. Sand is insoluble.

Light
We get light from the Sun, candle, fire, torch and lamp.
1. The **Sun** gives us **light** throughout the day.
2. When the **Earth** turns away from the Sun we get **night-time**.
3. We switch on **electric** lights in our homes when it goes **dark**.

Push and pull
1. pull, 2. push, 3. pull, 4. push

Gravity pulls
On the Moon you would weigh six times less than you would weigh on Earth.

Friction
high friction - sandy beach, muddy field
low friction - ski slope, ice-skating rink

Can you sink a plastic bottle?
Water pushes up on the bottle. The bottle will sink when it weighs more (or is denser) than the weight (density) of the surrounding water.

Submarines have tanks that can be filled with water to make the submarine sink or emptied of water to make the submarine rise.

Ship shape
Dolphin, stingray, shark, eel
Shape **C** is the best shape

In orbit

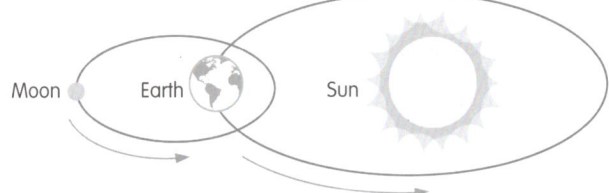

The Earth **spins** at an angle on an invisible axis. It takes the Earth 24 **hours** to turn once on its axis. This gives us **day** and night. The part of the **Earth** that turns towards the Sun has daytime. The part of the Earth that turns away from the Sun has **night**-time.